D0529030

GLASGOW'S DANCING DAFT!

Jimmy Brown

Richard Stenlake Publishing

© 1994 Jimmy Brown
First Published In the United Kingdom, 1994
By Richard Stenlake, Ochiltree Sawmill, The Lade,
Ochiltree, Ayrshire KA18 2NX
Telephone: 01290 700266

ISBN 1-872074-52-9

Printed by
Adlard Print & Typesetting Services
The Old School, The Green,
Ruddington, Nottinghamshire NG11 6HH

This book is dedicated to the memory of my friend, the late Bert Macdonald.

My thanks are due to Mary Aldrich, Chris Hayes, Rona Liaola, Jimmy Miller, Ken Sargeant, and the staffs of the Mitchell Library and Springburn Museum for their help and encouragement in the production of this book.

The publishers would also like to thank the staff of Springburn Museum for their help with picture research for this book.

By the same author:

Springburn to Inverurie
Harry Tate's Navy

INTRODUCTION

From the hornpipes, jigs, strathspeys and reels that enlivened the heels of Tam o' Shanter's witches down through the strict tempo times of Victor Silvester to the discos of the present day, Glasgow has always been a great dancing place. At one time the city was host to eleven commercially run palais that existed solely for the purpose of tripping the light fantastic, plus innumerable reception suites and smaller district halls, all of which resounded to the sounds of mirth and dancing each Saturday night.

Writing from a unique standpoint, as both a semi-pro musician and a keen dancer, the author relives the times and the characters of that pre-television decade immediately after the Second World War when Glasgow was, quite literally, plain dancing daft!

1

A Rerr Baun

In March 1946 I returned to my native Glasgow after wartime service with the Royal Navy Patrol Service. Pre-war I had been a keen dance music and jazz fan and I was soon taking it up again with others like-minded such as Tommy Caldwell, who worked beside me in the LMS Railway, and Bert Macdonald, who had been in my class at school. Bert had been in the Boys' Brigade Band attached to our school and before he was called up to the Army he worked in local semi-professional bands on trumpet. Tom Caldwell and I spent most of our precious gratuity money on a pair of Boosey & Hawkes 'Regent' clarinets and signed up with music teacher Harry Denmark for lessons. I knew a good pianist, Harry Bruce, we picked up a semi-pro drummer called Bob Wills, and before you could say Jack Robinson we had a band – of sorts!

Anywhere we could find people willing to allow us the use of their front rooms we would meet for practice. practice and more practice. Soon Tom Caldwell bought an alto sax and me a tenor and we started slogging our way through the dance band orchestrations of the day.

The Glasgow dancing scene of those days was really something. There were eleven commercial palais in the city where folk went first and foremost to dance. The strict licencing laws of the time did not allow drinking on the premises – a cup of tea or a soft drink on the balcony, maybe, but definitely no alcohol – so with little to cause any diversion it should not be surprising that Glasgow folk got the name of being the best dancers in the country – or anywhere else, for that matter! The ability to step it out with style and grace came as natural to your average 'keelie' as the famous Glasgow patter.

But throughout its history Glasgow was always a great dancing place. Even in the hungry thirties when not many folk could afford the luxury of indoor dancing, 'clabber' dances sprang up in the smooth, tarmacadamed streets south of the Clyde. Music was usually provided by an accordionist while some more organised affairs ran to drums and saxophone or trumpet.

But the real Glasgow dancing craze started after the First World War. One after another commercially run halls were opened, culminating in the huge Dennistoun Palais, where you could even dance with evening-dressed professionals for a small fee.

In any hall where two or three could gather together Saturday night hops were organised. Dancing styles evolved gradually from the French quadrilles through the hornpipes, jigs, strathspeys and reels that enlivened the heels of Tam o' Shanter's witches down to the latter-day quick steps of Victor Silvester.

But the style that became Glasgow's own was known as 'Select' dancing. Where the name came from is lost in obscurity, unless it was meant to suggest that select dancing was a cut above the rest. The steps followed a strict sequence, as opposed to the more tolerant rules of Modern dancing, and any couple departing from the laid-down routine were quickly pulled up by their fellow dancers and advised to 'keep tae ra figure!' Certainly the organised movement of the dancers round the floor made for fewer collisions, and this must have been a consideration as many of the patrons of select dancing were sturdily built. Especially the middle-aged married women, who seemed to predominate. Men were very much in the minority, possibly preferring the attractions of the pub, and their spouses danced with each other. Select dancing was very much a social get-together for lonely wives in the days before telly and bingo and tea and buns were usually laid on by the management.

Saturday evening papers carried columns of small ads giving details of these suburban dances, including the names of the M.C.s. These were invariably identified only by their first names – 'Bill and Jessie', 'Fred and Jean' etc. Informality was the keynote. But the M.C.s were very much in control and any lady who declined to dance without what the M.C.'s thought to be good reason was sternly asked to leave.

The Second World War saw a massive increase in Glasgow's dancing. The big palais opened in the afternoons to cater for servicemen on leave and Green's Playhouse introduced a big-band policy featuring the famous London broadcasting bands.

Joe Loss brought his band to Dennistoun Palais for one night in 1939 and the resultant crowds were so enormous that mounted police had to be called out to control them. Loss offered the management of the Albert Ballroom in Bath Street a 60/40 deal to capitalise on his undoubted popularity with the Glasgow dancers but this was declined. Then he approached Green's and got a booking to bring his band to their Playhouse Ballroom at Christmas, 1940, for a four-week season. His reception was truly phenomenal with no less than ten thousand paying customers recorded in one week. His initial engagement was extended to six weeks and he returned to Green's every Christmas and New Year for the next seventeen years.

Oscar Rabin from the Hammersmith Palais in London followed, bringing with him a Novachord, a primitive type of electric organ. This was too heavy for the lift at Green's and had to be oxtered up the ten flights of stairs to the ballroom by the squad of burly chuckers-out. It would be churlish to suggest that the smallness of Oscar's tip had anything to do with it, of course, but on the way back down the stairs at the end of the engagement something slipped and the Novachord crashed down several flights and was extensively damaged.

Harry Roy's band was next and after that most of the other big London bands queued up to play for what were generally regarded as the most discerning dancers in the country.

On more than one occasion, Joe Loss combined the Green's Playhouse job with a stage appearance at the nearby Glasgow Empire. This involved the musicians emerging from the stage door of the Empire in West Nile Street and running up to Green's, instruments in hand and with their stage make-up still on. Drummer Jackie Greenwood had borrowed a second kit so we who gathered to watch the fun were disappointed when he emerged carrying only his sticks.

Another time thieves broke into Green's and stole Joe Loss's evening clothes. Replacements were not readily obtainable and comedian Jack Anthony, who was appearing across the street in the Pavilion Theatre, offered the loan of his full Highland Dress. Joe Loss favoured a most athletic style of conducting and the kilt got waggled more during the rest of that engagement than it ever had before.

This dancing boom was still going full blast when we returned from the forces and there was plenty of work going for small dance bands.

Bert Macdonald, Harry Bruce and Bob Wills had experience as semi-pros and before long they were agitating for us to look for work.

Our first engagement was in British Railways' Ambulance Hall at Kilbirnie Street in the south side of Glasgow. We were all a bit nervous – even Bob Wills who was inclined to put it on a bit in view of his previous experience – but all went well and I felt a glow of pride when I overheard two committee men agreeing that we were, indeed, 'a rerr baun'

2

The Embassy Quintet

Next Tommy Caldwell secured us a short-term Saturday night residency in Baillieston Miners' Welfare Hall where we gained valuable experience playing for larger crowds.

Dancing was regarded as an essential part of wedding receptions in those days and we began to pick up jobs for trios at these functions – usually Harry Bruce on piano, Bob Wills on drums and me on sax. But we realised we had a lot to learn and Harry toiled away taking us through rough 'head arrangements' of all the likely material we might be asked to play. Apart from the usual quick step, slow fox trot and waltz routines we had to be ready for requests from the Old Time and Select catalogues. Anything from an Eighsome Reel, Dashing White Sergeant, Gay Gordons, Pride of Erin and St. Bernard's Waltz, through to such obscurities as the 'Gipsy Tap' and the 'Breakaway Blues'. Fortunately, most of the tunes were interchangeable in this musical jungle. But you had to be careful with the select dances which were usually taken at just above slow fox trot tempo. Some used 24-bar choruses and others 32-bar and heaven help you if you got them mixed up and left the dancers stranded with one foot in the air at the end of a number.

Other points to remember were that the Empress Tango, for example, had to be played at slow-fox-trot tempo while only one tune was ever played for the first round – Who's Sorry Now? Then there was 'Burlers' Own', very popular out Baillieston way. Required music for this was Moonlight and Roses played at quick step tempo and nothing else. We had a few orchestrations but it would not have been a practical proposition to carry round a complete library for everything we might have been asked to play. We all had good ears and provided we knew the tune we could usually busk our way through anything unusual that came up.

The quick step was the most popular dance. Usually every second dance was a quick step, and here we displayed our jazz repertoire. All the old standards like 'Jazz Me Blues', 'Darktown Strutters Ball', 'The Sheik of Araby', 'Who's Sorry Now?', 'At The Woodchoppers' Ball', and so on. We also applied a jazz treatment to anything we thought might benefit from it like 'Bobby Shafto' and 'When You and I Were Young Maggie', while at Christmas time we gave numbers like 'Jingle Bells', 'Come Landlord Fill The Flowing Bowl' and 'Good King Wenceslas' a going-over that might not have pleased their original composers!

For slow fox trots and waltzes we featured the tenor sax on such smoochy ballads as 'Laura', 'I'm in the Mood for Love', 'All The Things You Are' and 'Come Back to Sorrento', giving the others the chance for a quick smoke. All in all we seemed to be producing the right sounds and between one thing and another our wee band began to acquire something of a reputation.

The Glasgow Vet College in Buccleuch Street gave us regular bookings and on our first night we were half-way through one of our orchestrations when the lights went out and the band ground to a discordant halt. Instantly Harry Bruce called out 'The Sheik in two flats!' and led us in with a four-bar piano intro and the emergency was over. After that we didn't bother taking any music up to the Vet College since the lights were out most of the time. Pee Wee Hunt's 'Twelfth Street Rag' topped the hit parade at this time and the Vet College students asked for it. 'Twelfth Street' was in our normal jazz repertoire, of course, but after we played it we got complaints that our Twelfth Street Rag wasn't the one Jack Jackson was featuring on his Saturday night radio show. We bought the record and copied the arrangement note for note and next time we went to the Vet College we had to play Twelfth Street Rag no less than five times one after another! The applause was marvellous but after a couple of weeks playing Twelfth Street Rag everywhere we went we were fed up to the teeth with it.

One Saturday morning I bumped into our drummer, Bob Wills, in West Nile Street. He had been playing every night at weddings out at the Marlborough, a reception suite at Shawlands Cross, he said, and was on his way up to Chalmers Wood, the agent's office, in West Regent Street, to collect his wages. I was duly impressed and accepted Bob's invitation to accompany him and have a pint afterwards. At Chalmers Wood's offices I waited outside while Bob did his business but after a moment or two a man appeared and invited me inside. There he said: *"Mr. Wills tells me you play tenor sax?"*

Bob was standing behind the man nodding his head vigorously so I modestly admitted that I did, indeed, play a little tenor sax.

"Are you free tonight, Mr. Brown?" was the next question.

Again Bob nodded his head so I admitted that I was free that night.

"Would you like to play with Mr. Wills?"

More nodding from Bob so I concurred and was handed an envelope containing £1.50 and booked for every night the following week. I couldn't believe it!

I was a bit worried – why should Chalmers Wood give me money so readily when they knew nothing about me? For all they knew I might be a complete chancer! But Bob Wills blithely assured me there was nothing to worry about and we parted after arranging to meet in the Bay Horse pub at Shawlands Cross that evening. I had no dinner suit so I borrowed my brother Frank's navy blue suit and bought a clip-on bow tie and thus equipped took a tram to Shawlands Cross that night.
As I left the tram I couldn't help noticing what looked like a picket line marching up and down in front of the Marlborough but when I mentioned it to Bob Wills in the Bay Horse he dismissed it as of no importance.

"That's just the regular band", he said. *"They're on strike"*.

"Strike!" I howled. *"You mean to say I'm a blackleg – a scab?"*

Bob tried to reassure me, pointing out that I had accepted Chalmers Wood's money and would have to play since I had already spent some of it. He said he would take the tenor sax in to the hall, since the pickets didn't worry him, so I let him go on ahead and a short time later approached the Marlborough with my raincoat well buttoned up and my head down. But the pickets were on to me in a flash.

"You goin' in there tae play?" they demanded to know.

I admitted it but assured them I did not know there was a strike on when I accepted the engagement and would not play there again while the dispute lasted. They let me pass at this and I went upstairs to where Bob was waiting behind his drums with a student-type sitting at the piano studying a piano-copy of a popular number of the day called 'A Gal In Calico'. Introductions over, I asked him what keys he liked to play in.

"Any key you like," he said and my heart sank as I realised we had a right one here!

Fortunately for me the wedding was one of those affairs where there were many speeches made and toasts drank and songs sung so that we weren't called on to actually play very much and when we did Bob Wills kicked up such a racket on the drums no one listening would have known whether we were any good or not. I escaped from the Marlborough that night with a sigh of relief and phoned Chalmers Wood's office first thing Monday morning to cancel all future bookings.

As I became known in that musical world I began to get work with other small groups but I was never really happy playing far away from Tommy, Bert, Harry and Bob Wills, all of whom, incidentally, thought my Marlborough adventure hilariously funny!

Calling ourselves The Embassy Quintet, we got business cards printed and launched ourselves as a full-blown semi-pro band. When we could command a six-piece we made it The Embassy Sextet and brought in a pal of Tommy Caldwell's, John Boult, on string bass.

A friend of Bob Wills', Freddy Douglas, was our first manager but I soon took over the business side while Harry Bruce and Tommy Caldwell looked after musical policy. Usually this meant buying the piano copy of whatever was popular at the time and working up our own arrangement at one of our practice sessions. Tom roughed out a short arrangement of the Johnny Mercer number, 'Dream', which we adopted as our signature tune. Fred Douglas and a pal of Harry's, Donald Fraser, together with my youngest brother, Frank, and his mates, gave us a hand to cart our gear around. Private transport was out on the grounds of expense so we had to rely on buses and trams to get about. The old Glasgow Standard tramcar was ideal for this purpose as we could get the big drum and bass fiddle onto the front platform beside the driver. Once Bert Macdonald and Chic Coffils and I were coming down Springburn Road on a Standard with Chic's bass drum up front with the driver. Coming round the sharp curve just north of Petershill Road the tram jerked the bass drum off and it went rolling down Springburn Road with we three in hot pursuit. Fortunately we caught it before it got run over!

Tommy Caldwell and I were keenly aware of our shortcomings in only taking up instruments in our early twenties and we went all over the place to get practice, joining such unlikely outfits as The Springburn Military Band and The Garrowhill Light Orchestra to make up for lost time. We also joined a rehearsal band that met every Sunday afternoon in a ramshackle hall up a close near Bridgeton Cross where you chucked two bob (10p) into the kitty and just took a seat. But anarchy prevailed here. The trumpet players seemed to predominate and they were all mad keen on the ultra modern American bandleader, Stan Kenton, so it was his rather difficult stuff we had to struggle through. One day we had no less than nine saxophones – five altos and four tenors – and I was the only man brave enough to tackle the first tenor part, so any semblance of balance went out of the window. I stood up and suggested we try a waltz or something easy to give us a chance but I was howled down and denounced as a traitor to jazz and the next Kenton copy was put up in front of me. This turned out to be 'Intermission Riff', which has a comparatively easy ride for the saxes, so I sat there quite happily while the trumpets screeched away up among what looked like a lot of telegraph poles on the music copy.

But our own Embassy Quintet still occupied most of our musical interest and we were all very disappointed when the first inevitable rift appeared in the lute. Our drummer, Bob Wills, still had connections with other bands from the days before he joined us and we were shocked when a deputy drummer turned up at the Vet College in his place one night.

The deputy drummer wasn't much good and we spent a very unsettled and unhappy night with him. So much so that we had a meeting afterwards and decided that Bob Wills would have to go. The band came first, before girl-friends, jobs or any other commitment, and since Bob did not feel that way about it we would have to find someone who did.

At this time we were active in the Glasgow Jazz Club which met in the Musicians' Club above the Bay Horse pub at the corner of West Nile Street and Bath Street every Tuesday night. The Club had been founded by three lads from the East End of Glasgow, Kenny Sergeant, Tom Haughey and Donny Ross. Record recitals and improvised jam sessions were the order of the day and talented jazz players like Harry Bruce and Bert Macdonald were welcomed with open arms. Bobby Orr was an early member, playing trumpet before he joined the Kirchin Band – he later reverted to his original instrument, drums, to become a session musician in London. Glasgow tenor sax and vibes man, Jimmy Feighan, was another stalwart and there were some memorable two-tenor sessions between him and Mickey Deans, an old pro who had played with the likes of Joe Loss, Jay Wilbur and Lou Preager. A youngster from Edinburgh turned up to stand beside Bert Macdonald while he patiently explained how to get this or that effect on trumpet. He turned out to be the famous Freddy Welsh in later years.

Perhaps the biggest star to appear at Glasgow Jazz Club was the American singer, Pearl Bailey. She was performing at the old Empire Theatre nearby and Tom Haughey talked his way into her dressing room with an invitation to come over to our club. Her manager attempted to veto this idea on the grounds that her contract did not allow it but Pearl managed to give him the slip and turned up at the Glasgow Jazz Club later to give us a night to remember.

Bassist Jim McHarg founded The Clyde Valley Stompers from the Glasgow Jazz Club. He invited Bert Macdonald and me to his first rehearsal but we didn't go back because we thought the band had no future. Maybe not one of our wiser decisions but we thought we had a better band of our own at the time and it certainly highlights our loyalty to the other members of the Embassy Quintet. It also illustrates our lack of skill in forecasting results – or, at least, Bert Macdonald's, for Bert was a born gambler and most of what he earned throughout his life ended up in the satchels of the bookies.

A regular on drums at the Glasgow Jazz Club was Davie McGregor and we signed him up to take Bob Wills' place in our band. We also recruited a singer, Donny McKenzie. Apart from his vocal prowess, Donny was an LRAM and his singing and playing sessions on the piano at the interval became a major attraction everywhere we went. With hindsight I should have scrapped the band to become Donny's manager, for after a couple of years with us he crossed the Atlantic to make it big over there.

Harry Bruce secured us a contract to play each Saturday night in a huge hall at the North British Locomotive Company's plant in Adamswell Street, Springburn. I larry was employed as an engineer at the NB Loco and the dances were run by the firm's Ex-servicemen's Club. Normally used for playing badminton, the hall was bigger than some of the Glasgow palais so we enlarged the band by bringing in Jimmy Whiteford on trumpet and shifting Bert Macdonald on to trombone, his natural instrument. We also made John Boult on bass a permanent member to bring the band up to a seven piece, plus Donny McKenzie on vocals.

These dances were a great success. All-ticket, they were sold out week after week and at times we had difficulty forcing our way through the ticketless mob when the taxi we could now afford to run us up from the Red Lion pub decanted us at the hall door. Trad jazz was enjoying a boom at the time, and with our new line-up we could give a pretty credible account of ourselves in that field.

But we were only being paid at the standard rate and with all this popularity we figured we should book a hall ourselves and maybe clean up. We tried it in the close season from the NB Loco dances but it wasn't a success. Trouble was, all the good halls were already booked and the few standing emply had little potential. We tried the Bridgeton Public and the Stepps Public and ran the Cambuslang Masonic on Monday nights for a spell but the profits were minimal.

So back to the NB Loco's Hydepark Saturday night dances we went at the start of the 1950 Winter season.

But by this time we had yet another drummer. Davie McGregor had to work late one Monday night and this left us without a drummer at all – a most uncomfortable experience.

Poor Davie. It probably wasn't his fault that he had to work late. But the band's rule was inflexible and he had to go.

Tommy Caldwell and I had been practicing in the back shop of a fish and chip shop in Dale Street in Bridgeton, along with two other sax pupils of Harry

Denmark's, plus two trumpet players and a drummer – Chic Coffils from Springburn.

Of all the drummers I ever played with, wee Chic was the best. His kit was broken-down and tied with string but the beat he got from it was wonderful. So Chic Coffils became our third drummer. The band sounded better than ever with Chic at the drums, although organising him became a bit of a problem, for Chic was inclined to dump his kit at the last hall he played in and often it became a hectic rush to find the hall and the hall-keeper in time for the next gig.

In July 1950, Airdrie Town Council booked us for one Saturday night at the Airdrie Town Hall – a prestige engagement – while their regular band had their annual holidays. A deputation came to hear us in action and all seemed well until they told us the band would have to be an eight piece. This was going to be a problem as since we had gone up to a seven piece we had scrapped written arrangements altogether and played head arrangements from memory. We thought about adding a guitar to the rhythm section but no-one suitable was available, it being the Glasgow Fair Holiday Fortnight. We could not add another front-line player without a lot of rehearsal and it just wouldn't be worth it for one night. Then I had a bright idea.

A young lad I knew had just bought himself an alto sax and clarinet and was coming to me for lessons. Let me make it clear at once that no way did I consider myself a teacher. If the truth were known it was I who needed more lessons. But music lessons were expensive and I knew enough to take my young friend through the elementary stages for a start, after which he could go on to a proper teacher. I made no charge for this but told young John Sands he could do me a big favour by turning out with us at Airdrie Town Hall. He was to sit beside me and anytime I lifted my sax he was to lift his – but if he blew one note I would murder him! A slightly bemused John Sands did as requested. No-one was any the wiser and the council declared themselves thoroughly satisfied with the band when we collected our wages at the end of the night. John Sands went on to become a professional musician, playing with the likes of the Frank Weir Orchestra, and I sometimes wonder if he ever remembered the time he was paid for not playing!

The arrangements were meticulous at Airdrie Town Hall. We had to report at 7 p.m., set up and tune up and leave the stage at seven fifteen when the doors were opened. The doors closed again at seven thirty with the hall packed. I suggested to the M.C. that we should get started but he said no, our starting time was 7.45 p.m. We started at seven forty-five and played till nine fifteen when we were called off for our fifteen minute break. Refreshments were supplied – Barr's Irn-Bru – and at nine thirty we went back on for our final set, coming off after playing The Queen – or King as it was then – at ten thirty on the dot. A shooting brake was laid on to run us the five miles back to the centre of Glasgow and that was that.

We must have impressed Airdrie Town Council despite our subterfuge in the sax section for next they offered us a contract playing every Saturday night in the open air for Old Tyme and Select Dancing. No chance of playing jazz there but the terms were good and we thought we knew anything they were liable to throw at us. To be on the safe side, however, we took Tony Jackson, a marvellous accordion player, into the band to make doubly certain. The contract stipulated that we got paid whether it rained or not and the first Saturday night it was teeming cats and dogs when we met at our unofficial office and assembly point, the Red Lion pub in West Nile Street, to catch the bus to Airdrie. On arrival it was still chucking it down so we merely collected our wages and caught the next bus back to town and the Red Lion. Same thing happened the next two Saturdays and we couldn't believe our luck. But then Airdrie Town Council gave us a week's notice and on the final Saturday it didn't rain and we had to play.

A dinner-jacketed M.C. was in charge and the things he threw at us had us completely flummoxed. 'Ladbrook', 'The Pride of the Monklands' and the 'Saltzburgh Quadrilles' are only three of the monstrosities I can remember at this distance and even with Tony Jackson's help we were struggling, especially when we found that the Saltzburgh Quadrilles had eight bars of the Marseillaise, the French national anthem, thrown in the middle somewhere. 'Pride of the Monklands' turned out to be the same as the 'Pride of Erin' so that wasn't too bad and somehow we struggled through the night although we weren't sorry when the M.C. called the last waltz around 10.30 p.m.

In those days dances had to end in time for the customers to catch their last bus home. Very few owned cars and taxis were out of the reach of the average man . So most functions started at 7.30 p.m. and terminated at 10.30 or 11 p.m. at the latest. Friday nights were late nights till 1 a.m. when the first of the all-night buses started to run.

Wages were £1.25 for an ordinary night and £1.50 for a late night. Union rates were a bit above but any time we tried to get our wages up the promoters retaliated by threatening to cut the band numbers – and there were always plenty of other bands willing to work for even less. It was a cut-throat business.

Our main booking at the NB Loco's Hydepark Badminton Hall continued to run to capacity week after week but as we entered 1951 the band began to break up. What with playing every Saturday night and some week nights, too, opportunities for rehearsal were limited – usually we just worked up a head arrangement of anything popular from Harry's piano copy before the dance started. Big Bert Macdonald and I were quite happy the way things were but Harry Bruce and Tommy Caldwell grew increasingly restless as the band seemed to be stuck in a rut.

Chic Coffils took off for the south after some domestic dispute, then our star singer Donny McKenzie emigrated to Canada, while Oscar Rabin turned up at Green's Playhouse minus a bass player and pinched ours. Next Tommy Caldwell left to join an all-reading band. We tried out various other musicians but something was missing and as the season ended Harry Bruce decided to leave us and form a new all-reading band.

We all remained the best of friends – indeed, I was honoured by being asked to be Tommy Caldwell's best man when he got married to Agnes in 1954 – but that was the end of the Embassy Quintet/Sextet/Septet.

A romantic moment at the Oddfellows Dance Hall, 1949.

Relaxing in the Red Lion pub in West Nile Street between gigs. Left to right: Frank Smith (pub manager); Ken Sergeant (president, Glasgow Jazz Club); Jimmy Brown (sax and clarinet); Hammy Gordon (pub customer); Bert Macdonald (trumpet and trombone); Donald Fraser (band roadie).

The Embassy Quintet at Bothwell Miners' Welfare 1949. Left to right: Bert Macdonald (trumpet); Tommy Caldwell (alto and clarinet); Ken Sergeant (president Glasgow Jazz Club); Davie MacGregor (drums); Donny MacKenzie (vocals); Jimmy Brown (tenor and clarinet); Harry Bruce (piano).
Jimmy Brown Collection

The huge Dennistoun Palais served the needs of Glasgow dancers for many years. Here a hopeful taximan waits for a fare as dancers leave at the end of a night's enjoyment in 1957.
By courtesy of The Mitchell Library, Glasgow City Libraries.

Billy McGregor and his Gaybirds played for many years at Barrowland Ballroom, a very popular venue for Glasgow's dancers.
By courtesy of The Mitchell Library, Glasgow City Libraries.

An early shot of Springburn's famous blind band, The Rhythm Aces. Left to right: Tommy Neilson (drums and leader); Duncan Campbell (trumpet); Bill Lewis (tenor sax); Alistair Brown (alto sax); Ian Smith (accordion). Tommy Neilson was partially sighted and Duncan Campbell and Ian Smith were fully sighted. Duncan Campbell went on to play with the famous Ted Heath Band and The Rhythm Aces recruited Davy Lipman (piano) after Ian Smith emigrated to America.
By courtesy of Springburn Museum Trust.

Dr. Crock and the Crackpots. A famous comedy band that was very popular with the dancers at Green's Playhouse Ballroom in the fifties.
By courtesy of John Willis.

20

The ex-RAF Squadronairs with the famous American singing group, The Merry Macs, at the BBC studios, London, 1949.
By courtesy of Jimmy Miller.

Harry Roy's famous broadcasting band were regular visitors to Green's Playhouse Ballroom.
By courtesy of Chris Hayes.

The magnificent Dennistoun Palais as it was when it opened on February 16th 1938. The building was converted into a supermarket in the sixties.
By courtesy of The Mitchell Library, Glasgow City Libraries.

The Plaza Ballroom

Dancers queue for a refreshing ice cream or lemonade at the Dennistoun Palais cafe in 1957. No strong drink allowed!
By courtesy of The Mitchell Library, Glasgow City Libraries.

The Embassy Quartet. St. Aloysius Hall, Hillkirk Street, Springburn 1952. Left to right: Bert Macdonald (trumpet); Jimmy Brown (tenor sax); Chic Coffils (drums); Harry McToal (accordion).

Jas Brown's Jazzmen. Left to right: Bert Macdonald (trombone); Jimmy Whiteford (trumpet); Jimmy Brown (clarinet). Out of shot: Bob Johnston (piano) and George Phimister (drums)
Jimmy Brown collection.

3

Free-Lancing

Although the break-up of the Embassy Quintet left Bert Macdonald and me without a musical base we still picked up odd gigs here and there, as did the others, for that matter. Harry Bruce played once or twice with a lad called 'B-flat Bertie' who had a group made up of accordion, drums and two alto saxes. Bertie played alto sax and, as his nickname suggests, he could only play in one key – B-flat. But he had plenty of work and Harry thought playing with him might be not be too bad, although the strain of playing all night in one key just about drove him up the wall.

In the end Harry suggested to Bertie that he should play a chorus in the next number in E-flat. But Bertie was deeply suspicious at this departure from what he regarded as 'the norm'.

"Alright", he eventually agreed, although with some reluctance.

"Just so long as you remember to come back on the scale!".

To Bertie there only was one scale in the whole wide world of music – and that was B-flat!

Meanwhile I picked up the odd gig with various small bands at dances and weddings. I never became a good reader but I had an infallible ear that took me through most musical situations without loss of face. These small groups were usually three-piece – accordion and drums with me on tenor sax – and the repertoire didn't vary much, although one booking at the Highlanders' Institute in Elmbank Street stands out vividly in my memory. A ceilidh band booked me because they expected to be asked to play some quick steps and other Modern dances in addition to the jigs and reels that made up the normal dancing fare at the Highlanders'. When I arrived I tuned up and took a seat after being introduced to the other members of the band, which had an accordion, piano, bass and drums line-up. The leader was the accordionist and I got the shock of my life when he stamped his foot twice and the band took off into some wild Highland air. No mention of tune or key or anything like that to me and the others had obviously been playing together so long they knew what was happening by instinct. With my ear I soon picked up the melody and joined in but the accordionist was playing into a mike and little could be heard of my contribution. The tenor sax is a fairly powerful instrument so I stepped up the volume a bit to achieve some sort of balance but when the accordionist noticed this he merely turned up the volume on his mike and I was back where I started. After that I merely went through the motions of playing till we came to the Modern dances when I took over.

Bert Macdonald had the odd engagement with the Rhythm Aces, a band of mostly blind musicians that played around Springburn a lot. Leader and drummer, Tommy Neilson, had some sight while tenor sax player Bill Lewis had what they called a 'glimmer', but pianist Davie Lipman and alto sax player Alistair Brown were completely blind. Bassist George Otley had normal vision and he drove the band about in his van. They were all top class musicians. Indeed, Alistair Brown won the Individualist's Award for clarinet at the Melody Maker Dance Band Competition in

St. Andrew's Hall above many sighted men. The band respected Bert Macdonald's ability as a jazzman and sometimes brought him in when they could justify the expense.

One particular night the Rhythm Aces were playing at the Lorne Ballroom in Hawthorn Street and the committee were out on the pavement to conduct the blind men up to the platform when they arrived. When Bert emerged from the van one of them took him by the arm and led him up to the platform. Bert said nothing but when he reached the stage he thanked the committee man and started looking round for a chair, much to the astonishment of his guide and helper. But this was typical of 'Big Bert'. as we called him. He was always up to some trick or other.

When we were at school we had a middle-aged music teacher called Miss Noble and Bert was the bane of her life. She used to put the tonic sol-fa modulator over the easel and call us out one at a time to pick out tunes with the pointer for the rest of the class to sing. When it came to Bert's turn he took us swiftly through the opening bars of Harry Roy's signature tune 'Bugle Call Rag' before Miss Noble realised what was going on and called a scandalised halt. Then she divided us up into sections for choral singing. Bert's voice was breaking and he could sing soprano and bass at one and the same time. She would put him in with the sopranos, whereupon he would do his Paul Robeson bit, and then when she came round listening for the rogue voice he would revert to his peerless soprano.

Called up to the army during the war, Bert was asked the usual question at his first camp about whether he could play any musical instrument? Bert said trumpet and they told him they had a dance band with four trumpet players already in it. They said that the band was rehearsing and told him to go and listen, and if he thought he was better than any of the four players they already had they would give him an audition. Bert did this and duly reported back that he did not think he was better than any of their existing players.

Then they asked him if he could play anything else and when he said 'trombone' they nearly got out the red carpet for him. Apparently they had been waiting and praying for the call-up to send them a trombone player since the war started, for just one thing – to play the trombone part in Glen Miller's arrangement of 'In The Mood', which just doesn't sound the same without a trombone in the final fading choruses. Bert explained that he had been taught his music in the Boys' Brigade and they only used the treble clef, whereas trombone parts were in the bass clef which he couldn't read. But they brushed his objections aside and made him sit at the end of the four trumpets just to play his bit when they came to 'In The Mood', which was very popular with the troops. Bert got heartily fed up sitting there every night waiting for his one-note concerto and tried busking or transposing the fourth trumpet part but the sergeant out front ordered him to be quiet. In the end he volunteered for the Mountain Regiment just to get away from this musical purgatory.

Big Bert Macdonald and I had been pals since we met at Provanside Senior Secondary School in St. James's Road in Glasgow. I was about the smallest in the class while Bert was undoubtedly the tallest, even at that age. I would have loved to have joined the Boys' Brigade Band but my parents couldn't afford to send me back into town in the evenings to attend the band practices so at lunch time I went round to Bert's home in Paul Street to listen to him playing the trombone while he boasted that he could play any tune I cared to name by ear.

Bert had a bad stammer and I still writhe with embarrassment when I recall our French teacher, Miss Watt, making him stand up and sing his answers on the theory that one does not stammer when singing. I could have murdered her! But despite his stammer – or maybe because of it – Bert was very popular with the ladies.

On nights when we missed the last tram we sometimes refreshed ourselves at the coffee stall in St. Vincent Street while waiting for the first of the all-night buses at 1 a.m. Bert's 6ft. 3ins. height acted like a magnet to the ladies of the night who haunted these places and one such asked him:

"You lukkin' furra wumman...?"

"Naw, hen," replied Bert conversationally.

"Ah'm lookin' furra pie..."

The lady of the night thought Bert was taking the mickey and gave him a terrible sherracking.

Another time we were playing at a dance when a blonde girl called Beryl turned up who I thought had her unwelcome eye on me.

"Kin you no' go doon an gie her yer patter and get her away fae me ...?" I appealed to Big Bert.

"Certainly," said Bert, laying aside his trombone.

"Anything to oblige!"

As it happened, the next dance was 'The Dashing White Sergeant' but I thought nothing of it as I slogged away trying to make enough noise to cover the absent trombone, all the while thinking charitable thoughts about my life-long pal, Big Bert, risking his bachelorhood by giving Beryl his patter. It was only much later that I learned what he had actually said to her. It was something like this:

'How's you an' Jimmy gettin' on," asked Bert.

"No sae hot," replied Beryl. "Ah don't think he's aw that keen..."

"Well, don't let that fool ye," Bert went on impressively. "Ah'm his best pal an' ah kin tell ye – he's dead nuts aboot you – never talks aboot anythin' else...!"

The big bandit! And me blowing my guts out at 'The Dashing White Sergeant' while he took it easy.

But as I say, Bert was always up to some devilment.

His mother had a shilling-in-the-slot electricity meter installed and when it got dark the first night she put five bob in it.

"That should do us a good while," she remarked to Bert.

A little later Bert strolled casually through the lobby and, with his great height, flipped the main switch at the meter as he passed.

"My God!" exclaimed Bert's mother as she groped around in the dark for her handbag.

"Five bob gone already! That damned thing's goin' oot a' here the morn!"

Another time at a wedding reception in the old Royal Restaurant in Duke Street at the top of Bellgrove – now long gone – Bert was strolling along a passage to the toilet when a side door opened and a wee man looked out.

"Hullo, big fella," he said. "Will you be ma' bodyguard?"

"Sure thing," replied Bert agreeably.

"But why do you need a bodyguard?"

"They're oot tae get me" whispered the wee man, who turned out to be the bride's father, and who had obviously drink taken.

"*Who's oot tae get ye,*" said Bert, looking round the empty corridor.

"*Don't know...*" replied the wee man.

"*But as long's you're ma bodyguard that's OK ... come in here ...*"

Bert followed him into an ante-room which was well stocked with bottles of whisky.

"*Here,*" said the wee man, handing Bert a half-pint tumbler nearly full of the hard stuff.

"*Get that doon ye ... an' mind – you're ma bodyguard!*"

Bert downed his generous dram and returned to the bandstand and it should not surprise anyone that he found it necessary to go to the toilet again soon after. Sure enough, he encountered the wee man once more and received another tumbler of whisky to ensure his continuing loyalty.

The rest of us on the bandstand couldn't understand what was going on. Bert seemed to have developed a very weak bladder and each time he came back from the toilet he was getting visibly Brahms and Liszt.

In the end Bert could stand no more of the wee man's murderous hospitality and locked himself in the toilet.

But weddings were always a bit of a hazard so far as the supply of alcoholic refreshment was concerned. Then it was the tradition for the bride's father to supply the drinks and the quantity varied considerably. I always liked the story about the time my music teacher, Harry Denmark, had a quartet playing at a rather posh do out Rutherglen way. The bride's father was M.C. and he came up to the bandstand in full Highland Dress to ask Harry:

"*What will we have for a start...?*"

"*Four halfs and four beers will do nicely, thanks,*" said Harry cheerfully. And he got them, too, for his cheek.

At another wedding reception a young lad in short trousers was dishing out the refreshments from a tray, but every time he came to our corner he shot across the hall and back up the other side, oblivious to our clutching hands. Bert thought he had the solution to the problem.

"*Here, son,*" he said.

"*There's half a croon. You see the band gets a good drink!*"

"*Thanks mister,*" said the boy, obviously impressed, for half-a-crown (12^1/2p) was a lot of money in those days.

After that tray after tray came straight up to the band, much to our embarrassment and the annoyance of the guests. It got so bad I was scared to move my feet in case I knocked a glass over.

"*That's enough, son, that's enough,*" Bert hissed out of the corner of his mouth as we chuntered through the programme but the little lad thought he was just being good mannered and the flow of drinks continued unabated until, mercifully, the supply ran out.

Chic Coffils returned to Springburn about this time so Bert and I joined him and accordion player Harry McToal in a quartet for local gigs. But work was scarce and matters were complicated by Harry's being a fireman on the railways with his awkward shifts. It was a nice wee band – any band with Chic Coffils in it just had to be good – but I had to leave when I received an offer to join King's Park pianist Gordon McGhee.

4

Gordon McGhie's Dixielanders

Gordon McGhie had a useful gig connection on the south side of Glasgow and before long I got my big pal, Bert, into the band too. In the early fifties trad jazz was still very popular so I convinced Gordon we should specialise in this and brought in Jimmy Whiteford on trumpet and George Phimister on drums from our latter Embassy days. Jimmy was a fine lead trumpet while George Phimister had been a full-time professional at the Berkeley Ballroom at one time. Both had carried on with Harry Bruce's new all-reading band at Hydepark but this venue had failed for one reason or another and they were glad to team up with Bert Macdonald and me again. If I place Chic Coffils first in the drum race it is only by a very short head. George Phimister was a thorough professional and he held the drum chair in our band for the rest of its existence. He could also handle a vocal and we featured him in the faster jazz numbers like 'Darktown Strutters' and 'When You And I Were Young Maggie'. I still played mainly tenor sax, my best instrument, but I could play enough clarinet to get by in the Dixieland numbers. The main advantage of these moves was that we could now get Bert Macdonald back on trombone, his natural instrument.

Bert was a relaxed, easy going lad who loved a drink and a bet and there is no doubt he could have gone places in the jazz world had he been so inclined. One Sunday night he met up with the trombone player from Sid Phillips' Band, who were in Green's Playhouse at the time, at the Stage and Screen Club, and the two of them traded choruses on the 12-bar blues for a solid hour, with only a piano and string bass for accompaniment. Possibly as a result of this, we got a phone call at the Red Lion pub soon after inviting Bert to join a band Lord Donegal was forming in London. This impressed Bert's mother a lot for she was a red-hot Tory and Lord Donegal stayed in the same street as Sir Winston Churchill. Politically, Bert stood somewhere to the far left of Leon Trotsky and at election time he persuaded his mother not to vote since they would only cancel one another out. Then he did the dirty on her by slipping out and voting when her back was turned.

But thankfully Big Bert did not go to London or anywhere else. He stayed with me then and for the rest of our time as semi-pro musicians together in Glasgow.

When we could afford it we brought in either Benny Dick, George Otley or Willie Wasson on bass. Willie was a rather elderly lad from Clydebank who played mainly with ceilidh bands. Playing with us was a revelation to him and I remember him saying wistfully:

"Ah aye like playin' wi' your band!"

Gordon McGhie was a fine piano player. He was also an expert card-sharp, although he didn't look like it with his brief-case and umbrella. Bert dubbed him 'The Man From The Pru' after an advertisement that was current at the time. On nights when we were killing time till the one o'clock night bus left George Square we sometimes visited the telegraph office at Glasgow Central Station where a friend of mine was usually on duty. The cards would come out for a hand or two of pontoon but Bert soon gave up playing with Gordon. He must have been cheating, for he always turned up pontoons, but we could never catch him at it no matter how closely we watched.

We always gathered in the Red Lion pub in West Nile Street before setting out to play and one night two of the regulars, Aubrey Smith and The Moose, were amusing themselves at our table with the Three Card Trick.

"May I have a go?" asked Gordon in his best King's Park voice.

The lads handed over the deck but soon gave up when they discovered that not only was there no Queen under the card they chose – there was no Queen at all among the three cards on the table although they had seen one there a moment before.

Aubrey and The Moose were frequenters of race-tracks and they did their damndest to get Gordon to go with them to clean up.

"Make a fortune," they promised him.

"Thanks, lads, but really I couldn't," protested Gordon.

"After all, I am organist at King's Park Church!"

He was also an accountant with the City Chamberlain during the day, which was another factor mitigating against any idea of going round the race-tracks with Aubrey and The Moose to coin it in.

As Gordon McGhie's Dixielanders this new band soon caught on. One New Year's Day we were booked to play at Hamilton Town Hall. There was a regular reading band booked for the main hall and we were the jazz alternative in the small hall. Bert and I took a bus out and as we were standing on the rear platform waiting to get off we were delighted to see a big queue forming as we passed the town hall. Our starting time was 7.30 p.m. and it was still only 7 p.m., so we went into a chip shop to buy cigarettes. The appetising smell persuaded us to sit down and have a fish supper each and as we shovelled in the comestibles I glanced up at a notice on the wall.

'Grand New Year's Day Dance', it said.

'Two Bands – Joe Bloggs Band and the Dixielanders'

All very nice, I thought, until I came to the starting time.

'Commencing 7 p.m. sharp', it said.

It was already seven-fifteen and here we were stuffing ourselves with fish and chips when we should have been on stage!

We hurried along and, sure enough, the straight band upstairs was doing a roaring trade while our hall was empty. But it wasn't our fault, as Gordon and the promoter afterwards agreed – we had definitely been told seven-thirty.

We soon got started and before long we had the whole crowd down with us shouting for all the jazz standards. It was a happy time for us, being asked for the sort of music we liked to play anyway, given half a chance.

If we were doing well at our level things were beginning to get a bit quiet on the national scene. After the war several new bands started up only to vanish again soon afterwards. These included Tommy Sampson's, Malcolm Mitchell's and Ronnie Scott's to name but a few. During the war the London West End hotels and restaurants found they could manage fine without their expensive orchestras, and without that base there were only the palais and variety halls to sustain the bands. Roy Fox came back from America to start up again despite fierce opposition from Billy Cotton, who never forgave him for stealing his complete brass section when he first came to London in the early thirties, but he didn't last long either. That doyen of pre-war leaders, Ambrose, found the going so tough he gave up and became a manager for singer Kathy Kirby.

But there were at least two successful new bandleaders – Ted Heath and Ken Mackintosh. Heath did one Green's Playhouse session that I remember but his music wasn't all that popular with the dancers. Ken Mackintosh went on the road after a long series of Saturday night broadcasts on the BBC Light Programme from the Wimbledon Palais. When he eventually arrived at Green's a queue formed at the door for the first time in ages. One of the street buskers who haunted the Red Lion, Gerry Mason, burst into the pub that night joyfully proclaiming that happy days were indeed here again as he depended on a regular supply of queues for his beer money.

Bert and I were specially interested in the Ken Mackintosh band since lead trumpet, Alex McGregor, had been in our class at Provanside School. Like Bert, Alex learned his music in the Boys' Brigade band and the two of them had played semi-pro together before Bert joined up. Alex played with the Jack Chapman Band at the Albert Ballroom in Bath Street before joining Tommy Sampson's new band in Edinburgh. From there he moved to Ronnie Munro's Band before joining Mackintosh. Alex and some of his pals in the Mackintosh band used to join Bert and me in the Red Lion for a drink before going on each night and through that we became friends with such as trumpet player Bert Courtley, singer Kenny Bardell and bass player Alan McDonald. Despite his Scottish-sounding name, Alan McDonald was pure cockney and I can still hear him say with a sigh as he rose from his seat in the Red Lion: "Got to go up there an' play that 'orrible music Jim."

Because of our friendship with Alex McGregor, Bert and I got into Green's free when the band was in residence. Ken Mackintosh knew that I was a contemporary of his lead trumpet and that I played tenor sax so he used to put on his latest orchestrations and ask me what I thought of them! Nice to be asked, although my musical knowledge was not extensive enough to qualify me for the role of critic in these matters, I'm afraid!

Down in Blackpool on railway business one Glasgow September weekend I went round to the Winter Gardens where the Mackintosh band were playing. The hall was packed and I was standing at the side of the bandstand waiting for my friends to come off before going for a quiet drink some place when Ken Mackintosh announced a Scottish Waltz and jollied the dancers saying:

"There's a lot of Glasgow folk here this weekend, isn't there? There's one there, anyway – Jimmy Brown!"

The spotlights swung round to me and it was a very peculiar sensation indeed. I was used to appearing on stage but usually behind my tenor sax and this was something else!

The Mackintosh band were in Green's when the great Count Basie Orchestra came to Glasgow. The British Musician's Union had barred American bands from appearing over here from the early thirties but a reciprocal deal had been worked out allowing the Stan Kenton Band to tour here in exchange for the Ted Heath Band going to the U.S.A. With the log-jam broken, other bands followed and now we had the immense privilege of seeing and hearing the great Basie band. Bert Macdonald and I took in the first house at St. Andrew's Hall along with our pals from the Ken Mackintosh band, and we could hardly believe our ears. Cane chairs on the stage with instruments laid across them but no music stands. Apparently the band's library had gone astray on the way across the Atlantic but this didn't matter since the band knew the book by heart! One of the idiot tabloids of the day learned the band were playing without music and put out a story that they were busking, or playing by ear! Renaud Jones was lead trumpet and he found that role so effortless he was playing with only one hand! The band's performance was a revelation to us and I counted it a great privilege when I was allowed backstage afterwards to shake the great man's hand.

I went back to Green's Playhouse with the Kenny Mack lot after the show and it was a very subdued bunch of musicians that took the stage there that night, I can tell you.

Big Bert Macdonald went off on his own and got roaring drunk before going home to throw his precious trombone into the midden. Fortunately his mother rescued it before the dustmen came round but Bert's actions spoke louder than any words of mine could about the magnificence of that wonderful band.

Meantime down at our level several floors below things were going well for the Gordon McGhie Dixielanders until Gordon dropped a bombshell by announcing that he had accepted a post at Abadan in the Persian Gulf and would be quitting the band game.

But he handed his gig connection over to me and the rest of the band agreed to carry on under my leadership.

5

Jas Brown and His Jazzmen

The band's new title, Jas Brown and His Jazzmen, was coined by trumpet man Jimmy Whiteford, who also made music desks bearing the name. But these were purely ornamental. We carried our libraries about in our heads. My obsession with jazz in my youth had led my chums to shorten my name, James, to Jas, a nickname that still sticks among some of my older friends to this day.

But my first task as bandleader was to find a replacement for Gordon McGhie. Fortunately I thought I knew just the man – Bob Johnston, a piano player who had booked me as a free-lance sax player in the past. Bob had a major qualification for the job in that he was the manager of a whisky bond in James Watt Street and we had some fun with this in the Red Lion when the other customers asked us who we had on piano these days.

"The boss o' a whisky bond," we would answer.

"But is he a good pianist?" they would persist.

"Listen," we would retort with mock indignation, *"He's the boss o' a whisky bond, isn't he?"*

But Bob was a fine pianist and on those occasions when he produced a drop of the hard stuff at a gig it was noticeable that the band played with a great deal of spirit!

The staff and other customers in the Red Lion always showed a keen interest in our musical activities. From the management's point of view we were ideal customers in that our time in the pub was short and our consumption rapid since we had to drink up and get to the job in a limited time. In return they were always pleased to relay messages and even look after our instruments and other gear. The Red Lion became our unofficial office and meeting-place when we were off duty.

Among the other customers were buskers from the Odeon cinema queue, who used to cash up in the Red Lion after the patient cinema-goers had at last been admitted to the final showing of the big picture. There were several accordion players among this group and one night I ended up playing the Odeon queue alongside them!

In my free-lancing days I sometimes picked up a gig from Neilly McCormack's music shop in the Cowcaddens. Neilly acted as a sort of agent and many a Saturday night I was sent out to play with bands I'd never met before. Usually at wedding receptions and the music seldom varied much – in any case my 'ear' always saved my bacon. One Saturday night Neilly had nothing for me so I was sitting in the Red Lion enjoying a quiet drink when a couple of these accordion players came in. They spotted me in my dinner suit with my tenor sax case under the seat so they started pulling my leg, suggesting that I couldn't do what they could do. John Barlaycorn gave me courage to refute this and before I knew where I was, I was out busking the Odeon queue in my dinner suit and silver-plated sax alongside the buskers in their professional rags. My cut of the 'take' came to five bob (25p), as I remember, but when I woke up next morning and recollected the antics of the night before I blushed at what anybody who knew me in the queue might have thought!

Big Bert Macdonald encountered these same two box players one night when he was coming into the Red Lion for a quiet drink. He got off his tram under the Hielan man's umbrella in Argyle Street and was intrigued to hear two Irish tinkers playing button melodeons on the pavement. Bert paused to listen – no musical snob he! The Irish tinkers were good so he suggested they should play outside the Red Lion and, maybe, pick up a bob or two, since the Red Lion clientele were quite discerning in their musical tastes. They had to play outside the Red Lion, of course, because any sort of musical entertainment was frowned on in the Glasgow pubs of those days. You had only to raise your voice to be chucked out!

The Irish tinkers did as Bert suggested, and he was basking in the reflected glory as their discoverer when the accordion players came in. Tough guys, they demanded to know who had brought the Irish tinkers to their door and Big Bert saw the danger at once.

"Nae idea" he asserted. *"They were there when I came in."*

Next some of the other customers prevailed upon the pub manager to let the Irish tinkers play inside, for it was a cold night, and this incensed the accordion players from the Cowcaddens even more.

"We never get tae dae that," they snarled.

Bert sympathised with them but when the tinkers were allowed to take up a collection that was the last straw, especially when they bought a large Scotch with their new-found wealth and planked it down in front of their benefactor, Big Bert, saying:

"There ye are, sorr. Ye're a gentleman, so ye are!"

"Whit's the idea o' that," growled the tough guys, one on each side of Bert.

"They've the same name as me – Macdonald," blabbered Bert.

"Irish tinkers called Macdonald?" queried the tough guys. *"Never heard o' that!"*

"Oh, aye." Bert lied desperately on. *"They fled tae Ireland after the massacre of Glencoe – it's in aw the history books!"*

Fortunately for Big Bert, the tough guys were about as ignorant about history as they were about music and he was able to make his escape up to the Bay Horse for the rest of that particular night's drinking.

One Friday night we had a late night out at Busby with a 1 a.m. finish. I borrowed an ancient 1935 Wolseley Nine from a friend and when we got there Bob produced a five-giller of the best. We all had a dram and I confiscated what was left on the grounds that I was the boss, I was driving and better not have any more, and if I wasn't having any more, neither was anyone else. The others protested mightily but I locked the bottle in the car and made them get on with it.

It was a long night playing from 8 p.m. until 1 a.m. with only one short interval, and we were all ready for a livener when we piled into the car afterwards. Bob sat beside me and put the bottle into the hole in the dashboard. As we left Busby we ran over a pothole in the road and the bottle fell out to smash on the floor of the car.

"*Oh dear,*" said Bob mildly. After all, whisky was something he handled every day and one smashed bottle was neither here nor there to him.

"*That's the bottle fell out and broke...*"

"*Ha, ha,*" chortled Bert from the back seat, at what he evidently regarded as a good joke.

"*No kiddin' Bert,*" Bob assured him gravely.

"*The whisky's all gone into the carpet!*"

"*Fur Pete's sake,*" said Bert when he realised Bob was serious.

"*Whit happened?*"

"*Jimmy drove over a bump and the bottle fell out,*" said Bob.

"*Broon*", roared Bert.

"*Kin you no' watch wherr yer gaun?*"

And he went on at some length until Bob defused the situation by saying:

"*Never mind. We'll go down to the office and get another one.*"

And so it was that we all ended up in Bob's office down in James Watt Street around two o'clock in the morning enjoying a wee refreshment.

Seated opposite the frosted glass door of the office, I nearly had a canary when I spotted the familiar outline of two peaked caps – the poalis!

Here we were sitting drinking illegally at 2 a.m. with a car outside reeking to high heaven with the stuff from the earlier broken bottle. I thought we were for the high jump this time and no mistake.

But Bob Johnston didn't turn a hair.

"*Good morning gentlemen,*" he said when the bobbies came in. "*Nice to see you.*"

"*Coot morning Mr Chonston,*" said the poalis, who were evidently a pair of Tcheuchters. "*We were chust passing and we saw the lights.*"

"Of course," said Bob. *"It's a great comfort to know you lads are always on the alert ... and now that you're here, what about a small refreshment?"*

"Well," said the poalis.

"Chust a small one then"

Off came the caps and before long a nice wee ceilidh was in progress that lasted till near dawn.

Bob Johnston ran a most hospitable ship down at James Watt Street with every caller receiving a generous dram. He sometimes had a quiet smile to himself when one of the carters would call on a cold morning and, having received his dram, would find to his well-feigned astonishment on consulting his delivery notes, that his call was really further down the street. Any afternoon I was on the loose I would usually call and discuss our band business over a convivial glass and one evening I was standing with him at the door watching his girl workers trooping past when a rubber hot water bottle fell to the ground with a squelch. This was a girl attempting to purloin some spirit in a bottle fastened beneath her skirt. Unfortunately for her, the undergarments weren't equal to the strain. No police were involved in these circumstances. Bob's firm paid out bonuses at Christmas and the Glasgow Fair and anyone dismissed for theft in between times just lost their bonus – and their job of course!

On the band scene our bookings came in steadily. Once we played a job we invariably secured the repeat booking. As a keen dancer myself, I always saw to it that our music was eminently danceable. I loved to play jazz but our first consideration had to be the dancers and each night we played a Victor Silvester session in strict tempo. Usually a quick-step, with me and the rhythm section featuring numbers like 'You're Dancing On My Heart", 'Dancing Time' and 'People Will Say We're In Love'. With George Phimister and Jimmy Whiteford able to do a scat vocal there was always a sense of fun about the band that permeated down to the dancers. After a slug at Bob Johnston's bottle I sometimes even assayed a vocal myself on 'The Sheik Of Araby', although in my case I parodied the words into I'm A Shreik Of Agony.

"You're no kiddin'," the rest of the band would mutter.

"Sit doon an' no' gie us a showin' up!"

Like every band, there were some things that became traditional, such as our playing one chorus of 'The World Is Waiting For The Sunrise' after 'The Queen' or 'Auld Lang Syne', to sign off on an upper rather than a downer. This went back to the early Embassy Quintet days – I think it was Harry Bruce who started it. Then we did a thing called 'Mama Don't Allow' where Jimmy Whiteford took the vocal in which Mama was said to have forbidden the performance, initially of jazz, and then of every instrument in the band individually, with the performer in question then standing up to take a chorus in defiance of Mama's embargo. Trumpet was left to the last when I took over while Jimmy did his chorus. We kept Tommy Caldwell's arrangement of 'Dream' as our signature but this was incorporated into something called 'Roon the band'.

There didn't seem much point in playing our marvellous sig-tune first thing when there was normally so few folk in to hear it, so we played it again later followed by each man in turn playing one chorus of a number of his choice. I always took 'I'm In The Mood For Love' while Bert Macdonald did 'I'm Confessin',' and so on. We were always a singing band, although our variations on the original composer's words seemed to veer towards the bawdy for some inexplicable reason. Peggy O'Neil, for example, had her character torn to shreds. The politest lines I can recall are: *"Does it for charity, sweet personality, that's Peggy O'Neil'.*

The dancers revolving past would smile up to see us joining in so lustily and it was just as well the noise of the band stopped them hearing the actual words being sung! One non-bawdy variation that comes to mind was Bob Johnston's lines to that rather insipid ballad 'No One But You'.

'No one but you, could mulk a coo, fur me the noo' Bob would carol from the keyboard in a version that we, at any rate, found more acceptable than the rather trite original.

Our first dance was always a quick-step, latterly our own version of the Glen Miller hit, 'Little Brown Jug'. A pal of mine, Charlie Darroch, secured us a booking for his office dance at the Cadoro in Union Street, against strong opposition from his fellow committee members who wanted to play safe by taking the regular house band, and when we started up Charlie and his fellow committee men were watching anxiously from the far end of the hall to see what we were like. Charlie's face lit up when he realised that his faith in us had been vindicated and we were booked that very night for the firm's next dance. We always gave good value for money, perhaps because we enjoyed playing together as much as anything else. With no changes in personnel the band improved steadily until it became a smooth tightly-knit unit that could please the dancers and still give a good account of itself in the jazz idiom when the chance presented itself. We were always good pals and I looked forward to the flow of patter on the bandstand almost as much as playing the music.

The palais scene, several flights above our level, was slackening a bit as we approached the mid-fifties. More and more the bands coming to Green's were small groups like Sid Phillips', Carl Barriteau's or Harry Gold's, whose numbers were augmented to thirteen or fourteen players with local musicians. We used to joke that the big band at Green's didn't vary much – only the guy out front waving the stick changed every fortnight! Joe Loss vanished into the London Hammersmith Palais for a long residency, as did Oscar Rabin to the Strand Lyceum. Lew Stone went into the theatrical pit business in London, while the ex-RAF Skyrockets became the permanent pit band at the London Palladium. The other RAF band, The Squadronairs, which had contained the cream of the country's young dance band musicians when it was formed in 1940, were still regular visitors to Green's but their attraction faded a bit as their stars like Jimmy Miller, George Chisholm, Tommy McQuater and Andy McDevitt left to pursue more lucrative careers as London session men. One band that played to full houses at Green's every time they came up was that unlikely combination, 'Dr. Crock and his Crackpots'. Green's knew they were taking a chance booking this comedy band from a BBC radio show, 'Ignorance Is Bliss', but their gamble paid off. Dr. Crock was really Harry Hines, formerly lead alto with Maurice Winnick's band. His line-up was a full brass section of three trumpets and two trombones, plus an electric organ and *two* drummers. One of the drummers doubled as a comic but the resultant beat was strong enough to satisfy even the fussiest among Green's patrons. Dr. Crock was shrewd enough to know that he had to provide acceptable dance music and this he did, with the comedy as an added attraction.

Mid-way through 1955 we received an offer to play at the Kingsbridge Hall, King's Park, every Saturday and all holiday Mondays. The initial contract was for a year at rates that were – at last! – slightly above union level. The Kingsbridge Hall was exceptionally well appointed with floodlights, microphones and a grand piano that Bob Johnston positively drooled over. The dances were run by a committee of local residents and we really had no option but to take the job, even if it meant sacrificing much of our other gig connection.

King's park was then a slightly toffee-nosed suburb of Glasgow – strictly a dry area with the nearest pub miles away at Polmadie. We always met in the Red Lion in West Nile Street and made sure we were adequately fortified against the rigours ahead before we set out – a fact that did not go down too well with the M.C., who was inclined to look askance at the bag, clinking merrily, that Big Bert Macdonald invariably carried in his other hand. The M.C. was also a strict-tempo fan, which made him an enemy of Bert's at once, since the brass section were out in that particular mode. Sometime every night the M.C. would appear at Bert's side of the platform to shout across to me: *"Give us some Silvester..."*

"Sufferin' suckatash!" Bert would mutter into his trombone mouthpiece, for he was a fan of the cartoon cat, Sylvester, and the M.C. would come round to my side to ask:

"Is he drunk again...?"

Not that it matter much whether Bert was drunk or sober. So long as he could stand up straight his trombone rang out with unerring accuracy.

The band was an outstanding success at the Kingsbridge, with the hall packed at every performance. We played six-piece with George Otley from the Rhythm Aces coming in on bass. Apart from his bass-playing ability, George was also a vocalist and we even worked up some singing numbers for a quartet of such barber shop ballads as 'The Wiffenpoof Song'. George's van also came in handy for running us back into town afterwards.

Bob Johnston developed dermatitis in his hands and for a spell we used Davie Lipman, also from the Rhythm Aces, in his place on piano. Every other pianist I ever played with always ran up and down the keyboard between dances, but not Davie. He just sat there with his hands in his lap looking straight ahead awaiting further instructions. When we came to the inevitable Silvester session Davie made that big grand sound like the two pianos old Victor carried, much to our astonishment. In fact, I had quite a job keeping the rest playing while Davie was with us – they just wanted to sit and listen!

But if we were popular with the dancers, the same could not be said about the committee. Our practice of bringing liquid refreshments from the Red Lion for the interval raised some eyebrows and it was drink that led to our downfall and the end of the band.

Bert had taken more than was wise one Saturday and when he appeared in the Red Lion he was well into orbit. We took a taxi to King's Park and left Bert in the local cafe drinking black coffee with George Phimister's helper while we got started without him. Bert's absence was noted by the M.C. with grim satisfaction, and I wasn't best pleased myself for I was proud of my wee band's reputation. But Bert appeared soon after, a bit pale, but otherwise compos-mentis. He stood at the back of the bandstand and I slewed round to ask him:

"You aw right...?"

Bert nodded, so I growled: *"Well, get the 'bone oot an gie us a haun!"*

"He says ah've no' tae get peyed." Bert said, nodding over to where his arch enemy, the M.C., was standing, arms folded and with tight lips.

"In that case NAEBUDDY gets peyed," I declared, silencing the band with one wave of my hand, something like that man did with London's traffic in the song. 'The Mountains of Mourn.'

"We'll just pack up and go home now!"

The M.C. and I stood eye to eye while George Phimister unscrewed a tentative high-hat, Bob Johnston started packing his music away in his briefcase, and the dancers stood round in couples wondering what was up.

The impasse only lasted seconds before the M.C. capitulated:

"OK," he muttered, *"He'll get peyed."*

Bert might have been out of order but that was an internal matter for the band and we would brook no interference from non-musical outsiders.

Bert duly got paid but when our contract expired a few weeks later it was not renewed and that spelt the end for Jas Brown and his Jazzmen.

We had sacrificed our gig connection to take on the Kingsbridge job and I, for one, did not feel like starting from scratch all over again. A complication was that the taxman had caught up with some of the lads and nothing blunted a semi-pro's enthusiasm quicker than having to pay income tax. The Kingsbridge committee carried on without us – but not for long. Attendances dropped to the extent that they contacted me again, begging me to come back, and when I refused they humiliated themselves further by asking for my advice. It says a lot for my powers of self-control that I was able to give a civil answer.

But I cannot really take all the credit because dancing patterns were going into a period of change. I noticed it when the younger set started shuffling round the hall, step-and-chassis, no matter what the dance was. Then one night we got a request at Kingsbridge for some 'Rock 'n' Roll'.

"Anybody know what 'Rock 'n' Roll' is?" I looked round the band.

All were baffled except George Phimister.

"It's just the twelve bar blues," said George. *"I accentuate the off-beat and you play riffs on the tenor."*

We did that and no-one was any the wiser but with hindsight it was another straw in the wind. The great Glasgow dancing tradition was on the way out.

One by one the big palais closed or went into cabaret or some other form of entertainment. Even Green's, the home of the big London bands, found it difficult to book name attractions. Some of the bands they did book seemed to forget that the prime reason for their existence was to provide music for dancing and I could hardly believe my ears when I heard bandleader Vic Lewis, who was on a Stan Kenton kick at the time, assert that picking the correct tempo for the music was more important than playing for dancing. They gave a Glasgow rehearsal band, 'The Beavers', a booking, and took on London drummer, Sammy Herman, for a residency, but attendances dwindled and eventually the famous ballroom at the top of the stairs closed down. A few attempts were made to resurrect the great days but nothing clicked and the building gradually became derelict until, on the morning of 26th October 1988, it was destroyed by fire. It so happened, I was staying in the Central Hotel in Gordon Street the night before, and when I heard the news on the local radio in the morning, I walked along to look up Renfield Street to where the firemen were playing their hoses on Green's Playhouse from the top of their ladders. I read afterwards that the building was in such a poor state the firemaster would not allow his men to go inside and the whole place was completely destroyed. A sad end to a venue with many happy memories for a lot of people.

6

What happened to the lads?

Most of the lads got married and gave up music, although Tommy Caldwell and Harry Bruce carried on playing into pensionable age. Bob Johnston died young, and Bob Wills, too, has gone to join the Great Bandleader in the Skies. I never played again in public after the demise of the Jazzmen but Big Bert sometimes got a blow although opportunities became fewer as musical fashions changed.

Bert never married, lodging with his brother Jim's family until they emigrated to Australia in the late seventies. His nephew, Scott, took the place of the son Bert never had and he liked to take him out on Sundays on the Corporation dumper truck that was his last job.

Scott unearthed Bert's wartime medals and polished them up, declaring proudly: *"Ma Uncle Bert's a hero!"*

"He is nutt!" scoffed Scott's mum, Julie derisively.

"Your Uncle Bert's just a big drunken bum!"

"No way," asserted young Scott loyally. *"Ma Uncle Bert kin play the trombone – you canny even blaw yer nose!"*

But there was some truth in what Julie said.

Bert lived mainly for the thrill of placing a bet, with the pleasures of the pub coming a close second.

One holiday Monday Bert and I were left at a loose end when the Red Lion closed its hospitable doors at two-thirty in the afternoon. We were playing that night so our instruments were in the pub office.

Inevitably, we ended up in the betting shop at the back of Killermont Street bus station. I could see we were going to be there for some time so I studied the lists of runners with the intention of placing a bet just to pass the time. I was not a betting man normally. I never could see the sense in it.

Selecting an animal called Bass Solo because of its musical connotation, and another called Frere Jacques, since Jacques is the French for James, I invested two bob (10p) on a win-double. The horses came in at long odds and I collected quite a few pounds, much to Bert's amazement and disgust.

"Look at that," he appealed to his fellow punters.

"A genuine eighteen carat mug – an' he knocks it off at the first attempt!"

"Quiet, Bert," I warned nervously. After all, there were quite a few unsavoury characters hanging around.

"See that pound you owe me? Well, forget it, and here's another wan. Ah', off. See ye in the pub at five." And I made my getaway pronto. Apart from the danger of being mugged, I didn't want to catch the gambling bug and end up like Bert – perpetually skint.

When Jim and his family emigrated, Bert moved into a single person's flat on the thirteenth floor of a high-rise block off Kingsway, near Scotstoun. I tried to keep in touch, as did his faithful sister, Rona, but he seemed intent on cutting himself off from family and friends. Anytime anyone called he was invariably 'out'. I wrote to him and usually managed to enclose a few quid, although I knew most of it would end up in the bookie's satchel. Even when I warned him I was calling, he was often absent when I got there.

But one Friday evening I did catch him in – sitting by the light of an oil lamp listening to a scratchy battery radio. He was broke with nothing in his flat to eat till he collected his next giro on Monday morning. I immediately stocked his larder and left him what I could spare in cash.

Apparently Bert 'forgot' to tell the DSS about a small pension he was receiving from his last job and they had reduced his benefit when they found out. Also, he hadn't paid his electricity bill so they cut him off. I alerted his sister, Rona, and between one thing and another, we managed to get him back on an even keel. A card electricity meter was installed and when I heard the juice was back on I sent him a cassette radio to help pass the time. For a man who loved music like Bert Macdonald did, to be reduced to a scratchy tranny was as bad as depriving a junkie of his fix.

But he survived these mishaps and even got measured for a new pair of glasses at a shop in Partick. His mischievous sense of humour was never dormant for long and when the attractive young girl assistant invited him outside to test the efficacy of his new specs Bert gazed intently west along the tenemented canyon of Dumbarton Road for a minute before observing:

"Great. I've never seen Ben Lomond looking so beautiful!"

"Ben Lomond?" said the lassie incredulously;

"Ye canny see Ben Lomond frae here!"

"Think big, hen!" advised Bert dramatically, *"THINK BIG!"*

But the next I heard from Rona was that Bert was seriously ill in Gartnavel Hospital. It so happened I was to be in Glasgow that week so I made the trip out to the hospital but when I got there I almost walked past my friend's bed, so changed was he. He had been suffering from diabetes and that had now given him gangrene in his right foot. A strange effect of his illness was that his stammer had almost disappeared.

I kept up the usual optimistic patter one does on these occasions until I asked him softly:

"*Do you ever think of the band days, Bert?*"

"*Aw the time, Jas, aw the time,*" said Bert, using my old and almost forgotten nickname, and there was an infinite sadness in his eyes that brought a lump to my throat.

Bert's right leg was amputated below the knee and he was accepted into the Princess Louise Hospital for Limbless Ex-servicemen at Erskine, near Paisley. It was a fair journey from my home at Inverurie, north of Aberdeen, but I made the effort and was pleased to find my old friend in better spirits.

"*It's just like bein' in the Army again.*" confided Bert.

"*But the physiotherapist's a right bampot. She says I'm the fittest man here!*"

We talked away until I just had to ask the old question once more: "*Do you ever think of the band days, Bert?*"

The response was the same:

"*Aw the time, Jas, aw the time,*" with the same sadness in his eyes.

I pushed my friend in his wheelchair round to a conservatory and left him there in the weak sunshine of an October afternoon, turning round to give a last wave to the man who had been my friend for nigh on sixty years.

We wrote during Bert's few remaining months of life and I responded to his request for a copy of Neil Munro's Para Handy stories by sending him a precious paperback from my library shelves. Bert said an old Highlander in his ward had suffered a stroke and just sat in a chair not speaking all day until he discovered they had a common appreciation of Neil Munro's stories about the immortal Clyde puffer, the *Vital Spark*. Bert managed to bring a smile to the old man's face recalling the episode of the time the crew of the *Vital Spark* enjoyed Chuckie Soup. He bucked up after that and the story of the Chuckie Soup went round the hospital to the extent that Bert even managed to get it on to the lunchtime menu.

I inscribed the book to my friend, quoting the second verse of Robert Burns' Auld Lang Syne:

We twa hae run aboot the braes
An' pu'd the gowans fine
But we've wandered mony a weary foot
Sin auld lang syne.

Bert Macdonald died peacefully in his sleep on the 28th of March 1990, aged 67.

Glasgow's Springburn Museum held an exhibition, "Glancin' At Dancin'," in 1991 that was an amazing success, with mountaineer Tom Weir, who had once been a semi-pro drummer in Springburn, doing the opening honours. I was there on the big night with my old friend Harry Bruce and others who remembered the great days of "ra dancin' ". The event was well publicised on television and radio and the museum followed on by holding an afternoon tea dance in the former North British Loco offices in Flemington Street, with the music provided by Davie Lipman and Alistair Brown from the old Rhythm Aces blind band, plus a drummer. Sadly, David Lipman died soon after but Alistair continues to entertain pensioners, playing piano now instead of his beloved sax.

Glasgow's great dancing days may now be slipping into the pages of history, along with Big Bert Macdonald and the others who were such an integral part of it, but there is no doubt whatever that when Glasgow was a dancing place it was just plain dancing daft!